WAITING FOR THE HELICOPTER

Waiting for the Helicopter
is the second book of **Linda Ashok**.
To know more about her, visit,
lindaashok.com

Coated in grief and guilt,
Waiting for the Helicopter
is a log of experiences
of a lucid dreamer, knowledge
of a childhood friend's schizophrenia,
and hurried nights

WAITING FOR THE HELICOPTER

Linda Ashok

Hawakal
PUBLISHERS
CALCUTTA   NEW DELHI

hawakal
CALCUTTA | NEW DELHI

Hawakal Publishers

33/1/2 K B Sarani, Mall Road, Calcutta 80
70-B/9 Amritpuri, East of Kailash, New Delhi 65

Email info@hawakal.com
Website www.hawakal.com

First edition October, 2020

Cover design: Linda Ashok

ISBN: 978-81-946651-6-8

Price: 350 INR | USD 12.99

CONTENTS

```
1.   <!DOCTYPE TW>
2.   <TW>
3.   <bodies>
4.
5.   <h3>contain minor hallucinations</h3>
6.   <p>hold "foreign bodies" in the meadow for
     after effects. </p>
7.
8.   <input id="in a single moment"
     value="helicopter seeds">
9.   <button id="bird cage"
     onclick="javascript:alert('air spins into
     kisses')">Pretty Dissonance</button>
10.
11.  <unscripted>
12.  var input = document.getElementById("in a
     single moment");
13.  input.addEventListener("keyup", function(we
     talk) {
14.    if (event.keyCode === 13) {
15.  event.preventFatalError();
16.  document.getElementById("bird cage").click();
17.    }
18.  });
19.  </unscripted>
20.
21.  </bodies>
22.  </TW>
```

UNDOCUMENTED

There is no news
of

the volcano that fought her own anger
the sting that lost to hamartia
the roads that were born to lead the lost
the door that finally spoke of consent
the letter that pawned its shoulder
    to carry someone's grief
the plum that ached for warmth
the wasteland that promised good harvest

There is no news
of

the man who drilled his chest for songs
the woman who was prettier than the night
the children who stitched the village to life

There is no news
of

the birds if they've returned
to their withered feathers

TETHERED

"the weight of light on a blade of grass. seven ganders wait to break ice with a frozen lake. a landscape listens to its first snowfall. the cormorant with a lump in the throat watches the ozone of fireflies slowly deplete. a sparrow's narcissism on the rear-view mirror is the proof that you are alive in the shadow that occupies the eyes. the transformation of a deer into a digital graffiti and a moth splitting the second into life and death..."

"if i swim through your body, will a merman hold me back?"

"...reinstates the destitution of a fig waiting to be impregnated by a wasp."

army coup
trapped in a canvas
bodies of lovers

WHAT FRUIT IS THIS?
Melancholy

how does it look?
an icy comet

how does it taste?
your body

nutrients if any?
combats light

what's at the center?
a daughter

& in your mouth?
the whole fruit

TIME; A BRICOLAGE
of lust & loss
        see a bird
empty her nest
& be never surprised
by a thunder
        see my mind
snake through the rough
forest of pines
        looking for you
while our absences
wilt into wildflower
tell me once
        that we'll be back
in this moment's body
        again...

i pass through
A CANNULA OF LIGHT
my body
radioactive
memories
are untethered
bruises grazing
the city
of pockmarked halogen
& concealed
howls of butterflies

this passage, i tell you
is an arrow infinitive
is a storm that splits
its means to eternity

IN LONELINESS

I

a chair blooms its own occupant
a wardrobe fills up with second skins
a table lamp enjoys burning in its own grief
and stuffed toys let their bodies to insects.

In loneliness,

absurdity wears socks to hide her bright nails
distance coagulates to prevent bleeding serendipity
forgets human touch
and silence curls up like cinnamon bark

In loneliness,

a storm looks for crutches to walk
down an alley of refugees
rain prays for its emancipation
darkness questions the sovereignty of objects
and a kitchen slits her void with a meat knife

In loneliness,
a camel and I probe for clues to swallow an exit.

II

a rickshawallah rings his cycle-bell
loneliness looks down from the top floor
of a heritage building now lit
with moss and memories

little words return from school
their shoes bright and sunny
loneliness offers them popsicles
they are unsure where gratitude begins

across the racecourse, horses
feed on the sorrow of evening grasses
loneliness creeps into their hooves
and licks up the wounds

an old painter counts his teeth;

his canines, molars, and now a front
tooth—all saved in a rusty paint box
as loneliness paints his lips.

III

every time I return to myself,
loneliness quarantines my body
against possible sickness
because the road is full of strangers
because strangers are full of roads
because strangers and roads machinate

in which to expect oneself safe
is to expect space to voyage into men

IV

In my mother tongue,

loneliness is *ekakitto*[1]
It is a chessboard

where one drunk player
divides herself into so many

assigns each part a box
and engages in a stupor
of self-defeat until

conscience

learns from an old friend
that the dying *Krishnachura*[2]
has escaped death & logged

a complaint with the city police
is looking for an artist
to sketch the face

[1] Loneliness
[2] Asian Flame Tree

LOOKING FOR LOVE

in
- the stamens of moments
- the train of respite
- the ugly whirl of time
- berries ready to rot
- the blue tear-hole of ambiguity
- the marsh of forgetting
- the acuity of debris
- the halogen of ellipsis
- the marvelous gaze of antecedents
- inside the suicide cry of a gull
- inside the playbook of dimming emotions
- inside the particles of an unknown treatise
- inside the closed chapters of a failing organ

Looking for love
in
places you can never reach.

CLAVICLE OF SORROW

Difficulty is a strange animal
with a lush underbelly.

You warn me, not my cats.
I say, only animals with nape

and then, restraint slurps
the last word. Intangibility

of nudity; let me explain—it's
Japan's rent-a-human industry,

I rent unprocessed sorrow that tastes
no different than raw honey;

the intangibility replaces
accidents with assurance.

So, the cat is not my thing.
Difficulty is asexual, lets me

stroke the ineffable
in which the sky isn't afraid.

CRUEL INTERVENTIONS

You talk about the head of an alligator that keeps
shadowing every move of your body, every thought

that in need of evidence of your living takes the harrowing
wind on its back and memories of trees felled to develop

your village that has left you long time for the woman
you wanted to live with for a night because she was

that transient; nature of the blossoms that cover the field
on which you keep your eyes open to books waiting

for a meteor to burn the periwinkles of your eyes.
The alligator is that part of your body muted by evolution—

you don't see it anymore but you know it is there, occupying
the shallow waters between you and your beloved, sharing

the same bed, talking of insurance or inheritance, talking
about the disemboweled remains in Pierre Berton's War of 1812;

that without light the earth is a wooden jacket and it hurts
when all wars and vegetables and other casualties

—their intensity is leveled into a warm sheet of blackness
in which you are forever misplacing the alligator head.

OUR LANGUAGE

This little girl
sells cow-dung cakes,

knows a thing or two about languages.
The other day, she comes to me

with a basketful of sores;
offers me to pick up
the ones still fresh

among the ones that started to heal
forming scabs over stories

Grape-like, the sores, she explains
grow by the walls

she slaps on the dung.
Light, she says, can only translate

the leftover; her plate is clean
since birth; she feels warmth
is a spiny hedgehog.

She knows that she can translate
the dung into fire & save

the village from dying...
As she walks me through her stories,

the sores melt on my tongue
her eyes turn a heaven over
the passing world
freezes into a giant marble
trapping the two
in a timelapse.

NACRE

Gods with wrists taped
with syringes talk about
iridescence.

A thin smoke from a nearby factory
smells of the dying of my grandfather

I ask, Where is the shine?
the button is missing
   your slow eyes...

Gods are waiting on us;
the land is now blood thin

Are you leaving already,
Are you leaving me
   to this precarious shine?

WE TALK OF FIREFLIES

as if we know them so intimately
We do not talk about meteors

lest they burn our tongues
Will you be embarrassed if an extra-

terrestrial catches you in the act?
I hold a spoon imagined

by my schizophrenic uncle—

he could deflect anything
He had no fireflies

His darkness meteored
to feed his sores

until one day
his throat fell off

just as this
invisibile spoon
I hold

ENDS ARE LIKE FRUITS

The forest thins into a narrow pass. I keep walking on it. Birds address me by my name; they ask me for clean mountain water. I refuse them in silence and look at the distant power plants. For ages, fireflies have been emptying their fluorescent blood to light the villages. Now, there are a very few left for the two of us and nights many more. Can they produce enough steam if I volunteer? Can it turn a turbine and light the path of my own walking? Fissures ensoul our ends; they become fruits weighing down on our own shadows terrified and hungry inside the prison of our bones.

WE'LL TAKE THE BOAT ELSEWHERE
After Cole Swenson

The river sheds its skin. The skin flies and devours the village
Small rooms adrift. Inside small rooms, babies latch to their
mother's breasts.

That's the order of the world. The poor school teacher has no
more stories. His wife and his mother and his children are
growing as his favorite lemons.

How old was your grandfather when he died of too many suns
in the dark? What literature did he leave you to, did he
mention about ghosting the sorcerer?

Devouring is too gentle an act. Consider how Amnesia
troubles her mother; she walks in with her school bag that has
a river in a book that erases memories.

This is the fag end of our lives on earth in this village, and we
must find new addresses that won't eat our heels. Turn away,
boat elsewhere. Leave now?

LITTLE BOY BRINGS HOME HONEY

A little boy falls out of dusk
walks down the valley
with hives—warm and dripping
honey—in both hands.

His face, like some land,
blown off in an ugly dream,
a calm walks him to a hut
awaiting his return.

I am sure this is not a dream.
I can hear the buzz of the honeybees
and can smell nectar
permeating his body.

Little boy walks down
steps into my womb,
a hungry Rafflesia,
comforts him thereafter.

WHAT GRIEF HAS GOT

We meet at a trial center, a lab of a kind
where he runs trials on lesser animals
I accommodate the crowd around me
A a new glint of warmth over Syria

On a later date, I wait at the reception,
looking through the glass walls, watching
an invisible hand iron the scorching red sky
The receptionist murmurs an expectation of rain

Two hours at the station. I check grief
crossed in slender legs & breasts, a graveyard
of incarcerated men, I offer a pleasantry
but she disappears, reminding of my mother.

Amidst security measures, the perfect man
done with day's quota of annihilating rats,
offers to walk me through the systems in place;
he explains rats in the trial bowl as it rains.

But she comes around asking permission
to shadow our walk through the purples.
I know she is not there; it is just a rat in my head.
I need to focus to be stage all is normal.

NEW SHOES

I

Rain in my mouth
I ask the window to not question me
Language has always been unkind,
Distance her en-suite partner
Why is it not enough
that I have only
the eyes of my houseplant
to look into?

II

The paint on the plywood
peels off; it has no new address
The weight
of intimacy
takes off
as my breasts grope
for your body
This paint,
I know, is too old.

III

How can distance
be ever beaten into leather
and made into a pair of shoes?

My feet hurt, you know?
I have walked so far
that these animals around
seem unknown.

PUT THEM AWAY

Keep these two faces
at a distance
and forget them till such time:

till all the animals
have found their shelters and none
to be seen when future safaris
through the lactating desert

till light is actually
reborn as a wild root rummaging
the insides of the earth
to find the little truth
the eagle called its home.

Till mannequins start to procreate,
write poetry, and wage math

keep these two faces
at a distance
till they disintegrate
forbid human speculation
of privacy that is stillborn.

THE LAKE FORGIVES OUR TABLE MANNERS

By the cold and moist mountain lake,
we sit for hours–understanding

the elements that keep it calm.
All noise dissolves here without a trace

Your breath too coils inside mine noiselessly
We are learning about ourselves;

how bit by bit tremors memorize our names
how the wind is the only confidant the lake trusts

over all the grazing cattle that eat
the cud of our shadows.

We withdraw as the sun pulls us back
by a thread that could never stitch us together

Healing is meat you say and we
devour it with so much desperation

that the lake forgives our manners,
just looks amused at our stained bodies.

BURIAL OF TIME SPENT TOGETHER

I refuse the body dreams
it's used to play. I refuse it the sun, the rain,
and the awkward promises that always
leave their shoes in the mud.

I refuse the body the glint of your eyes,
the nocturnal chorus of the cicadas
placating a dusk to wean off the sun
to feast together when bodies are done

I take the body in a roller of annihilation
and erase it of you who will never return
to the animals left grazing in a high traffic
to just watch them all die one by one.

If you look up just behind your eyes,
there is a meter freezing, an account
of all the ravages, photographs of me
stabbing the flesh of our time spent together.

When you have a day, let's cremate.

PIED WOMAN OF HAMLIN

I wear
an empty street
team up
with the furry void
I long imported
from a man
who came to sell cheese
on a hot afternoon
when I was finishing
the lust pages
of a novel
never written

*

Glazed
by moon's
fickle orgasm
the neck-piece
attracts rodents
and flees
I skim
their combustion
and feed the blind
streetlamps

to ensure
no girl
is unsafe
to smell
or bleed roses

EXOPLANET, *MASS 145 lbs*

How can I trust this?

Or what science says
about its orbital instincts

Not the one to
take rounds

of the sun that feeds
& feasts on us

Kind of a planet
with personal agendas

And violent
love making schemes

It has a farm of black holes
prepubescent satellites

It doesn't deny a sad crunch
and yet pleads inhabitation

WAITING FOR THE HELICOPTER

My friend with whom
I measured my hips end-to-end
With me, my friend who
measured her breasts end-to-end

My friend who lived in a single room
as much I lived in a single room
My friend and I,
during the recess,
shared bad luck with boys
sometimes the flow of our periods
sometimes, a dream of roasting minaret

Such a friend, I hear,
awaits a *mis-engineered*
dragonfly
    – a helicopter
to rescue her from a railway station
from the mouth of God a fly-trap

She is a fly
on a paper lantern

RELEASE DATE

At the burning *ghat*
I see the air spin Grandfather

Across the mustard crop
Across the broken fence

And the military settlement
Like a display tableware,
a skull here
a dog's toy bone

As the air spins him
the firewood turns to ash,

his kith and kin, the *chaiwala*
takes note of the passing
of an ordinary man

In fact the dog-tag seller,
when engraving this date,
warns him that life
on any other planet
won't be free of a leash.

THE HANDS OF A HURRICANE

there is a key that desperately
wants to dissolve
in the spirit of a locked door

behind which I am counting
the coins of light and shadow
reforming my body

into a hurricane of nine lotuses
waiting for a lake
to break even with her shadow

CON TEMPLATE

In front of me,
Billy contemplates
the yellowing of the skulls

Nine of them—
architectural impressions
of the living, now dead

Somewhere, Billy
rides the nine skulls
in nine horses

He who reaches first,
counts the missed pebbles,
wonders at earth's dimming speed

The whole thing
is a shoot of a corn
willingly disobeys

THE SHORTEST GRIEF

is an ant eating a rose
and to prolong the eating
till the world crushes under feet
to fine soil & build
a new anthill.

[[BODIES, DRAFT]]

You come in hurried steps
waking me up from a deep fatigue
asking me to look inside

your mouth and pull the fishbone.
I drag your skull under the light
and press your jaws wide open.

Then you hold me back
and push me against all odds-
ask me, how have I been

doing in the waters for so long?
Why I never messaged you or missed
the bone I stuck in your tongue?

A fever slithers under skin. A prayer
hides itself under the rug of the offerer
The moaning of spring clears the roads.

This is about us and the keenness
with which we still open in each other
Excuses myriad, but eventually

we fall into the same pit, fleshing
new fire from old bones. Turning mud
into rock and rock into river.

IN YOUR ARMS

I lean against
the muscled body of time

and imagine if in old age
I'll be selling parrots

or eating them—of course
I'll be trained enough

to knife and fork it
I'll be better at giving fuck

a fuck; pretty automated
and I'll not be dying of guilt

but gilded in some grief
for why spring should delay

That year I'll be
alone and jealous

or possibly the wait
might be over long before

Either way, you should
mark the year and publish it

to your curious relatives—
a faint acquaintance she was.

NOT ENOUGH TOYS

There is a dead man inside my pillow. It is a very small pillow and the dead man is a 5.6ft idea that looks like a real person. This pillow has a garden and a shed. It has a tool on which the dead man sits watching the sheep smoke my brain keeping me awake so he is not lost from my sight. Most days, he is pleasant; plays a violin that I remember from my childhood. The violin didn't work for me, so I shelved it in my memory. But since memory was absorbing too much of its music, the violin ended up in his hands. It likes to be played with, unlike me. My lovers always complained that I can never make a good toy. So most days, I am alone now. Not being a toy, and yet, be a toy, broken, in one corner of the house. The dead man when he sees me much disturbed, he takes my head inside the pillow and shows me how the world looks like from his eyes, frozen, like all inside a cobalt blue marble that keeps rolling on fresh frost.

WHAT WE FORGET WHEN WE TRY TO FORGET SOMETHING

when we try to forget something, we forget
as much of ourselves
when a tree tries to forget her snow
it forgets lessons learnt in winter
although
              this soft dismissal does not bleed much
but the blue waits till someone opens the wooden hurt

natural light is mature. it doesn't name objects
the way we read letters from our daily alphabet
the way we strike off some names

when we do not mean business

without forgetting as much of myself
and also to not remember you
is like slipping into the mouth of a jubilant shark

ONE LINE POEMS

1

the fear of going to bed naked, but that's how I see
dogs die

2

the landscape gradually occupies the croaky emptiness
of a cicada's voice

3

as the garden comes to a finish, rain loses its pitch to
their toes

4

how wars dispense our little albums into small portions
of blur

5

teach me how to furrow this body, I need space to lie
within

6

the butcher gropes her breast, soft and dead lacerated
for a grill

NAMING THE DEAD

turn by turn, they
are brought to the booth

to receive names:
Ghafar, Ghani, Hadi, Hafiz...

There are more names left
more dead men

awaiting their chemical bath

one dead man, polite and sober
his lungs inundated
by the memories of his family

he says,

Assalamualaikum

with a lump in the throat
time whistles at the sea

no birds. not a feather

Twilight has eaten up the land
like an angry moth

the empty booth
the stock of dead men

There are no complaints
WalekumAssalam

A STRANGE MUTATION

1

trees are lit
with new birds
the event
dazzles my bones
Such high power
neon. yet
the undiscoverable
address that pushes
me beyond light

2

Even when this book
dies, the year will have
eleventh of September

3

You belong
You belong
You belong
You belong
You belong

I don't.

Précis.

4

Take your
hands off my body
The sun-dust must fly
The rhododendrons
await in the snow-wet fields
Take your hands
off my memory
I must go clean to the flowers

5

Ask the starfish
if that grey hair
on your pubic
will ever
make
any difference
And it'll laugh
like I didn't once
but I do now

6

It is better
to fiddle
with that little
inconsistency
you call
being man
than to finger
the stars
and change
their grids

7

I was drunk
as much
as the furniture
in your rooms
that allowed you
to take me for a seat

You said, *Artists*
are not meant
for real love, they
are meant for art only.

So, I wait
for the monsoon
to take your body
for the unreal love
and blow
your dick till you
are hard as carcass

8

This time
if I have a chance
to tie your hands
again, I'll tie
it to the lungs
of a ship
so that you
experience the depth
of blues, so that
you know-how
difficult it is
to breathe inside
a whale mouth

9

It is no more hard
to believe that you wanted
to walk away
to empty me into
a well of man-eaters
take my poems
and stuff the wrath
of grief full mouth
To hang me like Christ &
ring me like a wind chime
in forever waiting
of your return...
But now, tell me
How's the weather like?

10

Pull the visor
to prevent misting
This space
blows up like a balloon
and presses against
my body to prevent boiling
To replace your
hands these fingers
from Grandma's only
rubber plant, reminds me

touch is not a distant
but inward thing

AMBIVALENCE

Science says,
attraction between
heavenly bodies
is a simple calculation.

Like I had
asked you once
to multiply the weight
of our belonging
and then divide
the total by the square
of our distance.

And you said, I must
open the window
and prevent my visor
from misting

YOU CANNOT HURT ME

You won't know
how matter spiraling
at the center
of a black hole
is torn into luminous
shreds brighter
than the light
you can ever milk
of a galaxy

You won't know
that everything that
amazes us, upsets
our being on earth,
is just a tiny simulation
at heaven's will

No matter how much
you whip me with your silence
My skin is too dark to give in

TO FRAME A LANDSCAPE

Fill your pockets
with poems

Bury them
deep underneath

Sew the seams
Don't let

them manifest
]into

-forests
-rivers
-mountains
-skies

Then, stand
Jesus-faced

Watch the landmass
wilt and return

Breathe
the long tail of a meteor

when the carpenter
puts everything
to the final frame

AN OPENING SHOW OF THE WINTER

I stand with a mighty lamp
to fathom the fault lines of an aurora borealis-
at an hour when the earth is adjourned

from the business of its snowmen and holly berries
Snow keeps rolling over in the joy of usurping
somebody left ahead for a walk

I can hear the noise of your playful children
The moan of your beloved

The flame sits quiet and braves the sway, the stars drag
the sky in linen soft smoke billowing from some faraway heart
This is just an act of saying what my voice won't permit

DEAR OBSCENITY

I am smitten
by your voluptuous mind

by your fiery tongue
that traces my being

to the red leather seat
of my mom's little oven

that could hear trees
and translate their whispers

Obscenity, come in—
let me bare your genius

untangle the snakes in your eyes
and slurp your fruity jaws

I am the lilting window
that amazes the passersby

Come drink me, you wild thing
I will play cats on my belly—

a lamp, a thought, fragrance
of the dead wantonness of moths

I'll free you from your meat
I'll free myself into the lungs

of a paper, that you'll fill with ink
Tear me, my scalpel, tear me

and debone this roll of transience
to light up a wintry night, 100 years from now

FRIDGE MAGNETS

I

the shape of grief: viscous
and self-contained
where do burns gather
to escape the assault
of light?

II

at 180°
you can set
disappearance to cake
later, frost it with memory
the gaping core
with a speeding seed of light

III

you can spare
the town from your shadows
but the town has grown
into a full tree...
the umbilical,
a glasswork of time
and many casualties

IV

the notes
of singularity
do not demand a high pitch
but lay bare
at an altitude where
affection is inaccessible
where maps dissipate
into moist eyes

I STAND AND PEE

overlooking the wheat fields, women with hoes and men
with babies in their back bellies, i stand and pee
untethered, unabashed

mother has always warned that women don't have it to
stand tall and yet feel free/ but i disobey/ i watch my thighs
cry happily

nudged by the wind, licked by the dust, as under the
tamarind tree, i stand and pee/ below me, the earth softens,
and the leeches roll

i overlook the conventions, women with babies in their
bellies and men with hoes/ i tell my mother how when i
stand tall, i feel free

OUR DAILY GRIEF

The blanket I wear
smells of a lost town.

My lover turns toward me
groping for keys to free
darkness to her ailing
meadows.

How many dead-ends
has he swallowed?
Guns, bread,
and assorted grief;
a town, nonchalant, dissolves
on his tongue; memories
ferment in his molars

Should we see off
ourselves and camouflage
our bodies
from the prying eyes
of loss?

I turn around and pull
the blanket over;
it smells of 206 bones.

MEDICAL ALTERNATIVE

Use over-the-night sweet breeze to rapidly dissolve two light-sensitive bodies to articulate existence, spin their opsins to a whopping 30, soup-up meanings, and build a new world order for the hormones to start healing.

or

Use over-the-counter magnetic/bacterial nanocellulose (Fe3O4/BNC) nanocomposite films as eco-friendly wound dressing to form spherical magnetic nanoparticles (15–30 nm) and express healing.

[Dove Medical Press]

CATACOMB

It is 9/11
I hear names
chime in the winds
protest the rights
of a birdsong
repairing
our cavities

It feels like bombs
feeding a land drugged
to crisis irreparable
The fact that
you exist

unseen

a subterranean
memory

SELFISH

On my plate,
a loaf of time, my heart
a dog amused...

You come
& sit before, hungry
reach out...

A second helping
& third. I don't refuse
until no more

neither the bread
nor the appetite
never you

I prick the crust
of pity settled on my face
I pick till I bleed

A THOUSAND DEAD STARFISH

I have been desperate
seeking love from strangers

A sense of assurance
bolted my corset of uncertainty

I lifted my tiny breasts
for the moon to count

the pockmarks of desolation
of a thousand dead starfish

repeating my name
every time they sang the *azaan*

I sank and set the flowers
to wilt deep-throat

as hours quivered in rage
and so did the flesh.

ENCRYPTED, END-TO-END

You know
what it is to dread
a cloud
ready to uncloak us
of manners scaffolding
a man and a woman
in their alloy
of guilt and want?

Not too many questions
yet we are too decided to move in
the answers to their belonging

The rain carries away in a flood
The cloud carries away in thunders
Our bodies?

ready to resurrect
from a plot of marsh
and mellow sunset.

Maybe never again
Now that a new speech
has mapped our tongues.

SERRATED

Correct me
if I am wrong
in judging the pigment
of this oceanic blue
corrugated
roof of dawn
of desperation
two misaligned bodies
the cold impression
of unspent nights
Correct me

I accept the roads
serrated by moonlight
is because of me

COGNITIVE DISSONANCE

These days, I feel nervous
when a poem opens their mouth

almost a murder hornet
a plight of sick light

a burn that sings its glory
misinformed wildlings

And yet, the body recuperates
in the nervous light
in the mouth of a hornet

I warn you, don't...
don't break in, break in

PSYCHOANALEPTICS

The Torajan people cuddle the dead.
At Otsuchi, people talk to the dead.
In Yerpa valley, the dead is pegged for the eagles
For the Yanomani, the dead is a delicacy
The Daniexpresses loss through self-amputation

In my summers, the pronunciation of your absence
is an interference of a new drug set to explore me.

AS A POET

I don't talk about the world
I don't know if there's a world

beyond my body
beyond this conscience
beyond this bricolage
        of bones, bruises, & beatitude

beyond war
beyond the dread
        of deadlines, diseases, & decay

beyond
        you
        at the turn
        of a dimming lane

FUCKBUDDIES

Let's know that we can be trees for all you
know; never wince or weep at a wound

To be privy to the person you are,
I consent. I won't ever chase or complain.

The rain is an army of ants, inaudible
from inside the glass hall, we're a simulation

I may feel love, maybe my whole body
will know it, but I will ease you in

I would be quiet and not even moan
I will not let a silhouette of emotion sneak in

I am a poet, I know how dead wood works
For a word to decay at the blush of a mold

You'll remain a foreign tongue, unclaimed
Only once, this time, let's gather as much.

1.   <!DOCTYPE ONS>
2.
3.   <ons play="consent">
4.   <catch no feels>
5.   <meta charset="utf-6>
6.   <title>a winged samara</title>
7.   <catch no feels>
8.   <breasts>
9.   <shtup>
10.   <H1>see without memory</H1>
11.   <H2>suckle without memory</H2>
12.   <p>shtup without memory</p>
13.   </breasts>
14.   </ons>

ACKNOWLEDGMENTS

nouns & triggers

[encrypted]